spot

OUTDOOR FUN

HORSEBACK RIDING

by Nessa Black

AMICUS | AMICUS INK

mane

saddle

Look for these words and pictures as you read.

stirrup

reins

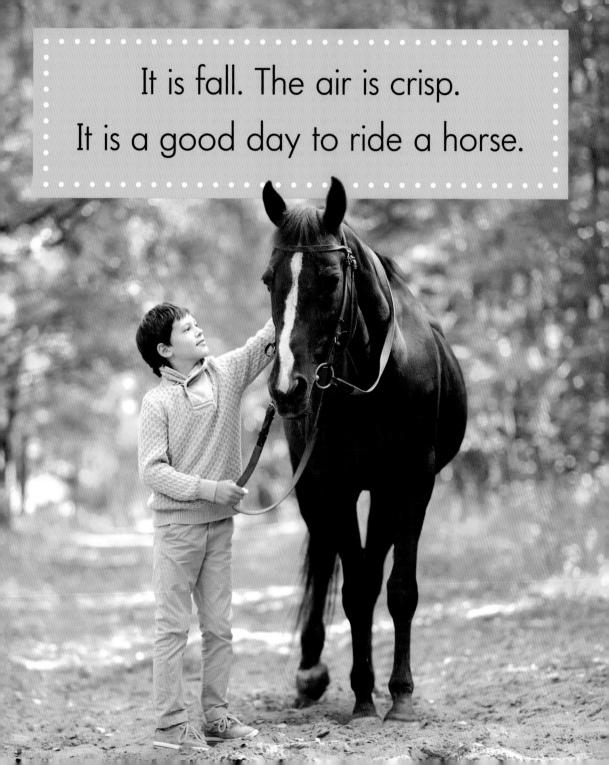

It is fall. The air is crisp.
It is a good day to ride a horse.

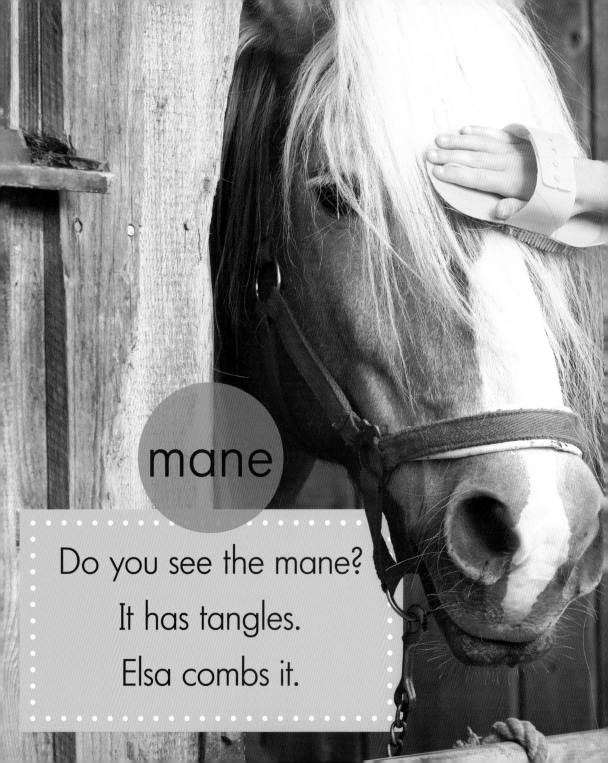

mane

Do you see the mane?

It has tangles.

Elsa combs it.

Do you see the saddle?
It is made of leather.
It is a seat for the rider.

saddle

Do you see the stirrup?
Noah's foot rests in it.

stirrup

Do you see the reins?
They help the rider steer.

reins

Giddy-up!

Claire's legs squeeze the horse.

The horse starts to go.

The horse jumps. It is a fun ride!

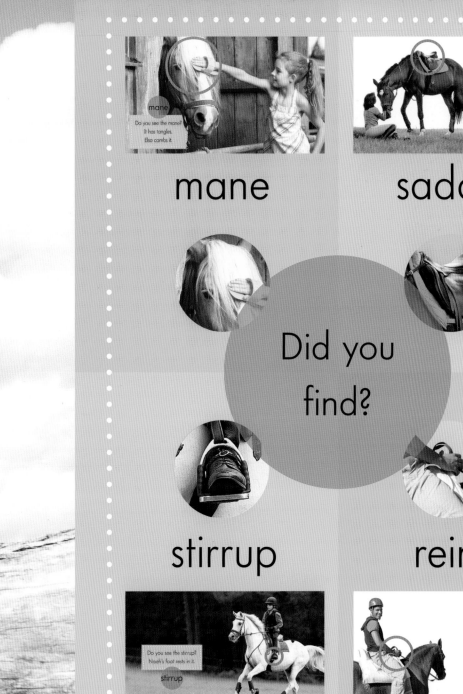

Do you see the mane?
It has tangles.
Elsa combs it.

mane

Do you see the saddle?
It is made of leather.
It is a seat for the rider.

saddle

mane

saddle

Did you find?

stirrup

reins

Do you see the stirrup?
Noah's foot rests in it.

stirrup

Do you see the reins?
They help the rider steer.

reins

Spot is published by Amicus and Amicus Ink
P.O. Box 1329, Mankato, MN 56002
www.amicuspublishing.us

Library of Congress Cataloging-in-Publication Data
Names: Black, Nessa, author.
Title: Horseback riding / by Nessa Black.
Description: Mankato, MN : Amicus/Amicus Ink, [2020] |
Series: Spot outdoor fun | Audience: K to Grade 3.
Identifiers: LCCN 2019003797 (print) | LCCN 2019005099
(ebook) | ISBN 9781681518534 (pdf) | ISBN
9781681518138 (library binding) | ISBN 9781681525419
(paperback) | ISBN 9781681518534 (ebook)
Subjects: LCSH: Horsemanship--Juvenile literature.
Classification: LCC SF309.2 (ebook) | LCC SF309.2 .B57
2020 (print) | DDC 798.2--dc23
LC record available at https://lccn.loc.gov/2019003797

Printed in China

HC 10 9 8 7 6 5 4 3 2 1
PB 10 9 8 7 6 5 4 3 2 1

Wendy Dieker, editor
Deb Miner, series designer
Aubrey Harper, book designer
Shane Freed, photo researcher

Photos by virgonira/iStock cover,
16; Westhoff/iStock 1; Rohappy/
Dreamstime 3; Altrendo images/Getty
Images 4–5; Cultura Creative (RF)/
Alamy Stock Photo/Alamy 6–7; Juniors
Bildarchiv GmbH/Alamy Stock Photo/
Alamy 8–9; Image Source/iStock 10;
Kostic Dusan/123rf 12–13; Zave Smith/
Alamy Stock Photo/Alamy 14–15

HORSEBACK
RIDING

Hong **KONG**

Lynn M. Stone

The Rourke Book Company, Inc.
Vero Beach, Florida 32964

PHOTO CREDITS
Courtesy Hong Kong Tourist Association: cover, title page, p. 17, 18;
© Keren Su: p. 4, 10; © Frank Balthis: p. 7, 8, 12, 13, 15, 18

Library of Congress Cataloging-in-Publication Data

Stone, Lynn M.
    Hong Kong / Lynn M. Stone.
       p. cm. — (China)
    Includes index.
    ISBN 1-55916-317-8
    1. Hong Kong (China)—Juvenile literature. [1. Hong Kong (China)] I. Title.

DS796.H74 S76 2000
951.25—dc21
                                                          00–038723

Printed in the USA

CONTENTS

MODERN HONG KONG

Hong Kong is one of the most important places in China. It is also one of the most important places on the entire **continent** of Asia.

Hong Kong is important because it is a major **port** on a busy trade route for ships. A port is a harbor where ships load and unload their goods. Hong Kong's port is large and deep. It is ideal for big, oceangoing ships.

Hong Kong is a major gateway city to China and the continent of Asia beyond.

Hong Kong is a territory made up of several cities, villages, and islands. Altogether, Hong Kong covers about 420 square miles (1,100 square kilometres).

Hong Kong is divided into three major areas – Hong Kong Island, the New Territories, and the Kowloon **peninsula**. A peninsula is a long, narrow piece of land that is surrounded on three sides by water.

The New Territories include part of a large peninsula and more than 230 islands.

With hills and mountains behind them, Hong Kong cities crowd the water's edge.

6

HONG KONG ISLAND

Hong Kong Island is a great rock rising from the sea. Its highest point is Victoria Peak at 1,815 feet (556 meters) above sea level. Part of the city of Victoria is built on steep streets halfway up Victoria Peak.

Hong Kong Island shelters Hong Kong's harbor from the waves and winds of the South China Sea. A tunnel under the harbor links Hong Kong Island with Kowloon.

Hong Kong's Central District is a hot spot for commerce and shopping.

KOWLOON

The city of Kowloon faces Victoria across Hong Kong harbor. Kowloon lies at the tip of the Kowloon peninsula.

Kowloon has a very small area, but a huge number of people live or work in Kowloon.

Kowloon couldn't spread outward because of mountains. But Kowloon has grown upward in tall buildings called **skyscrapers**.

Night falls on the busy streets of downtown Hong Kong.

Victoria Peak offers birds-eye views of Hong Kong.

The Jumbo Floating Restaurant in Aberdeen is a favorite eating place for tourists to Hong Kong.

THE NEW TERRITORIES

The New Territories are behind Kowloon to the north. They form Hong Kong's 17 mile (27 kilometer) border with the rest of China.

The New Territories are home to most of Hong Kong's factories and some of its skyscrapers.

Except for Lantau, the islands of the New Territories are small and have few people. Some people take ferry boats from the islands to work in Kowloon or on Hong Kong Island.

Apartments and gardens share space on Lamma Island In Hong Kong's New Territories.

HONG KONG HARBOR

Much of Hong Kong is rugged and hilly. Hong Kong's most useful natural feature is its wide, deep harbor.

About 12,000 big ships cruise into Hong Kong's harbor each year. (Hong Kong also has a busy airport.)

Hong Kong is a gateway to China. Many of the goods leaving or entering China pass through Hong Kong.

Chinese shoppers visit open markets in one of Hong Kong's villages.

PEOPLE OF HONG KONG

Hong Kong has about 7 million people. Ninety-eight of every 100 are Chinese.

The Cantonese type of Chinese is spoken in Hong Kong. But many people, especially business people, also speak English. Hong Kong was controlled by England (Britain) for more than 100 years. England returned it to China in 1997.

Chinese lanterns seem to be everywhere during Hong Kong's Mid-Autumn Festival.

Today, Hong Kong has a special place in China. The Chinese government lets Hong Kong continue to trade freely, just as Hong Kong traded under British rule. Hong Kong has its own type of money, too.

China has agreed not to bring its **socialistic** system of government to Hong Kong before the year 2047.

Free trade with outside nations helps keep Hong Kong's harbor busy.

VISITING HONG KONG

People from all over the world visit Hong Kong. They enjoy Hong Kong's warm climate, its restaurants, beaches, and shops. Hong Kong is famous for its watches, cameras, and clothing.

Visitors also enjoy the harbor views, seaside drives, trips to Victoria Peak, and the Ocean Park Marine Aquarium.

Lantau and other islands have parks and wildlife **reserves**.

Another favorite place to visit is the walled village of Kam Tin.

GLOSSARY

continent (KAHN tun ent) — any one of the world's seven large land masses, including Asia

port (PAWRT) — a seaside city where ships load and unload goods

reserve (ri ZERV) — a place set aside to protect wild animals and plants

skyscraper (SKIE SKRAY per) — a very tall building

socialistic (SO shu LIS tik) — referring to a government that has a large degree of control, in one form or another, over the group it governs

FURTHER INFORMATION

Find out more about Hong Kong with these helpful books and information sites:

- Nance, Lui Fyson. *Hong Kong.* Raintree Steck-Vaughn, 1990
- Stein, Conrad. *Hong Kong.* Children's Press, 1998

Hong Kong Tourist Association on-line at www.hkta.org
China on-line at www.mytravelguide.com

INDEX